FIVE 5 FINGER Piano

Disney
LATEST MOVIE HITS

ISBN 978-1-5400-2809-9

Disney Characters and Artwork TM & © 2018 Disney
Disney / Pixar Elements TM & © 2018 Disney / Pixar
All Rights Reserved.

HAL•LEONARD®

Visit Hal Leonard Online at
www.halleonard.com

Contact Us:
Hal Leonard
7777 West Bluemound Road
Milwaukee, WI 53213
Email: info@halleonard.com

In Europe contact:
Hal Leonard Europe Limited
Distribution Centre, Newmarket Road
Bury St Edmunds, Suffolk, IP33 3YB
Email: info@halleonardeurope.com

In Australia contact:
Hal Leonard Australia Pty. Ltd.
4 Lentara Court
Cheltenham, Victoria, 3192 Australia
Email: info@halleonard.com.au

Evermore
from BEAUTY AND THE BEAST

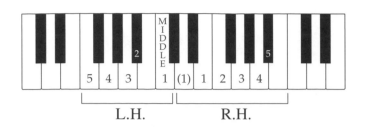

Music by Alan Menken
Lyrics by Tim Rice

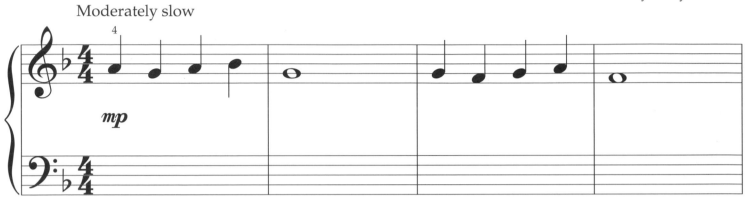

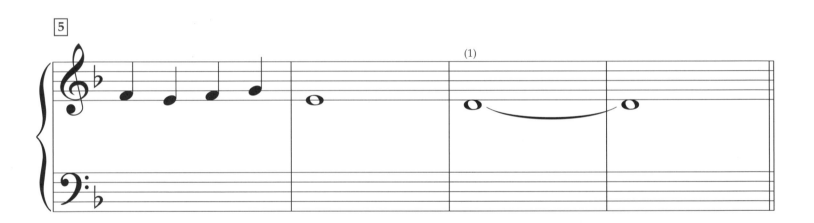

Duet Part (Student plays one octave higher than written.)

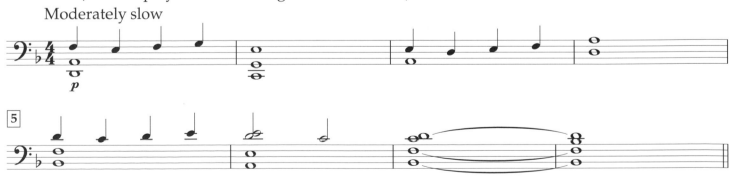

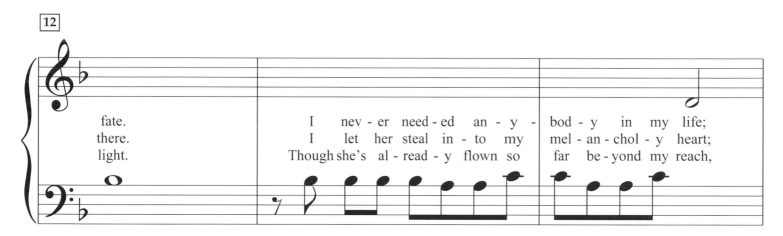

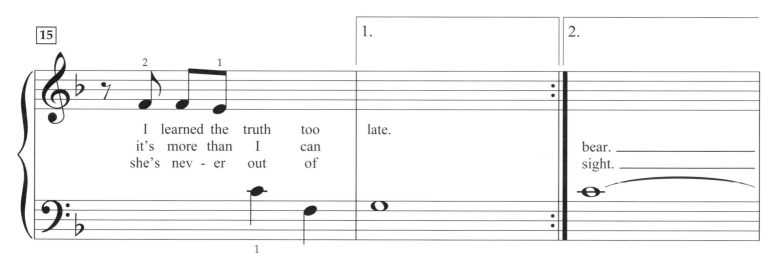

Now I know she'll nev – er leave me, e – ven
Now I know she'll nev – er leave me, e – ven

as she runs a – way. She will still tor – ment me,
as she fades from view. She will still in – spire me,

calm me, hurt me, move me, come what may.
be a part of ev – 'ry – thing I do.

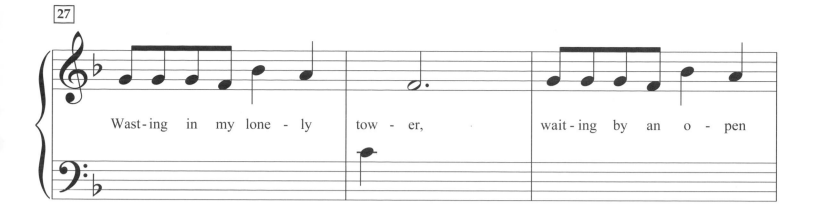

Wast-ing in my lone - ly tow - er, wait-ing by an o - pen

To Coda ⊕

door, I'll fool my-self she'll walk right in,

1

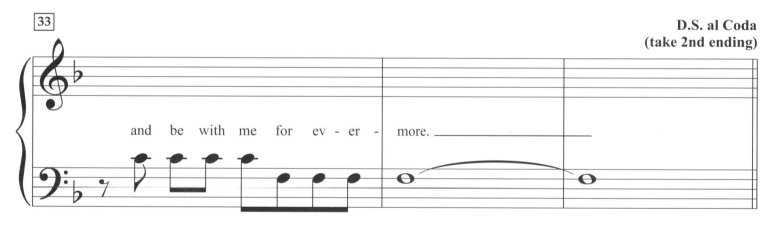

D.S. al Coda
(take 2nd ending)

and be with me for ev - er - more.

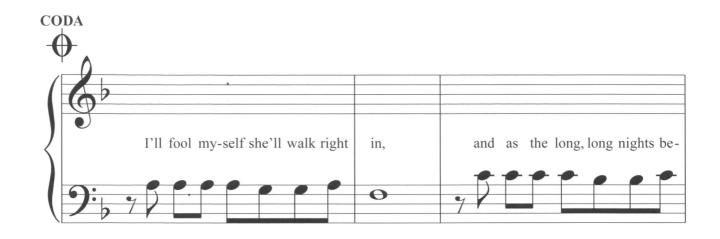

I'll fool my-self she'll walk right in, and as the long, long nights be-

39

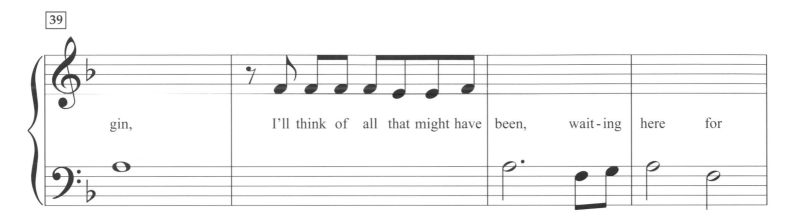

gin, I'll think of all that might have been, wait-ing here for

43

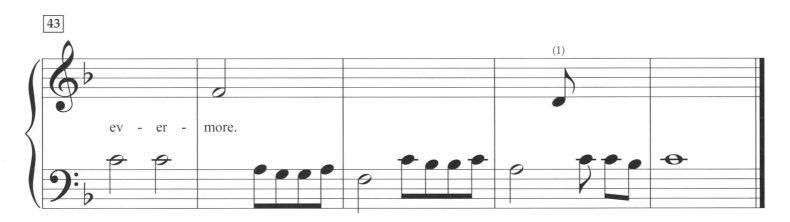

ev - er - more.

(1)

Do You Want to Build a Snowman?
from FROZEN

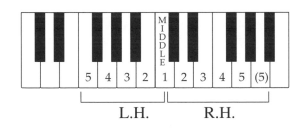

Music and Lyrics by Kristen Anderson-Lopez
and Robert Lopez

Do you want to build a snow - man? ___ Come on, let's go and

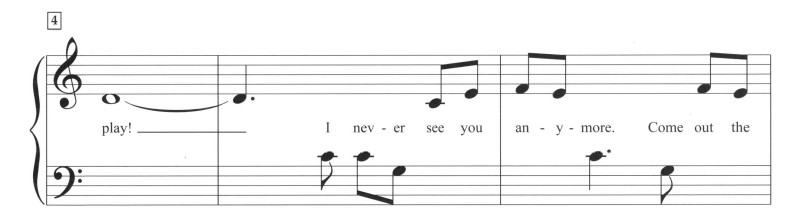

play! ___ I nev - er see you an - y - more. Come out the

Duet Part (Student plays one octave higher than written.)
Moderately fast

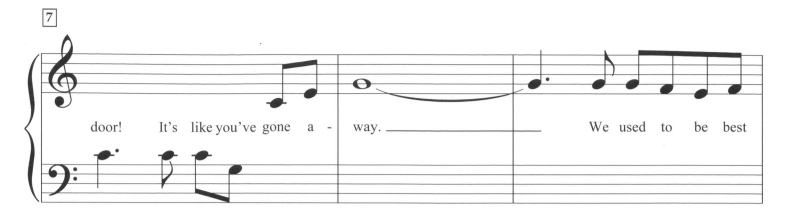

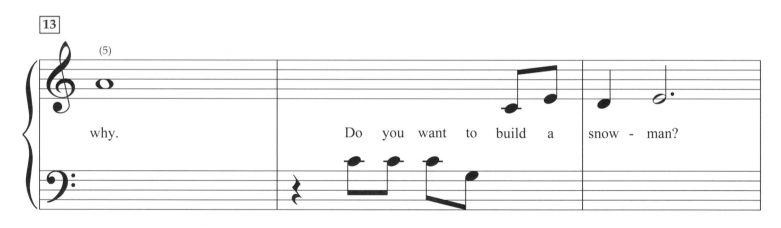

It does-n't have to be a snow-man.

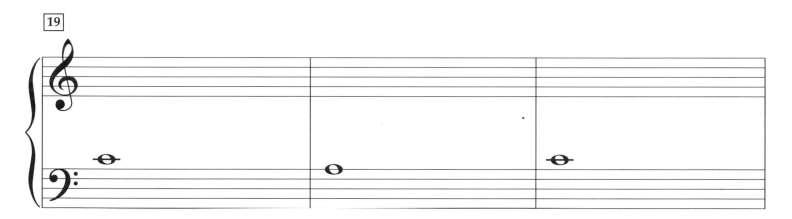

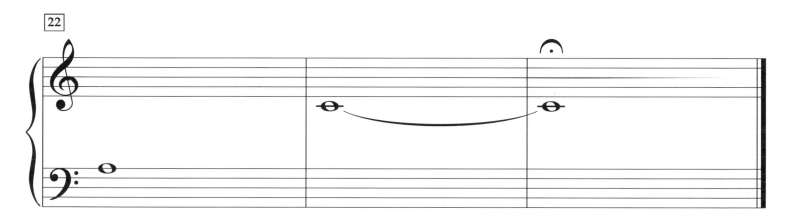

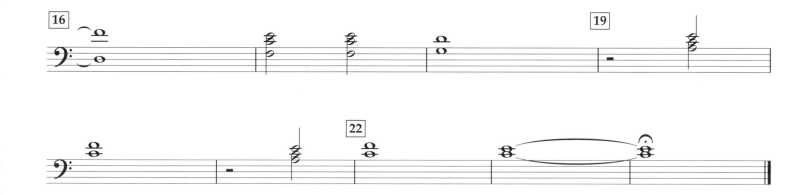

How Does a Moment Last Forever

from BEAUTY AND THE BEAST

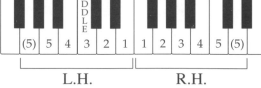

L.H.   R.H.

Music by Alan Menken
Lyrics by Tim Rice

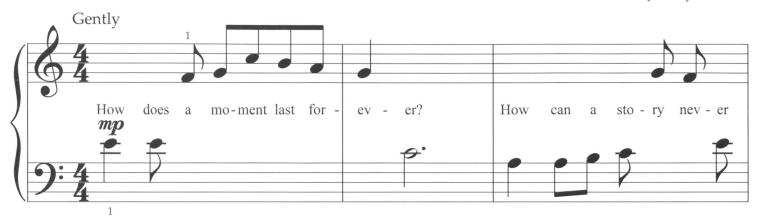

How does a mo-ment last for - ev - er? How can a sto-ry nev - er

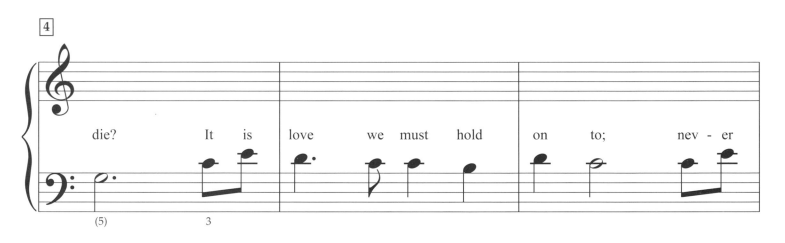

die? It is love we must hold on to; nev - er

Duet Part (Student plays one octave higher than written.)

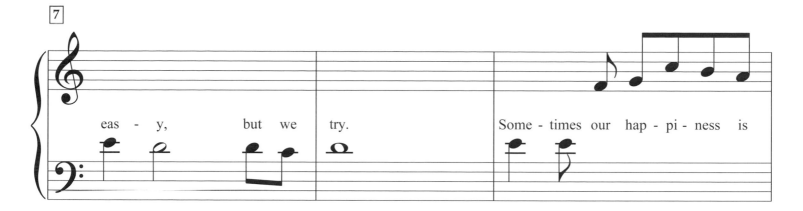

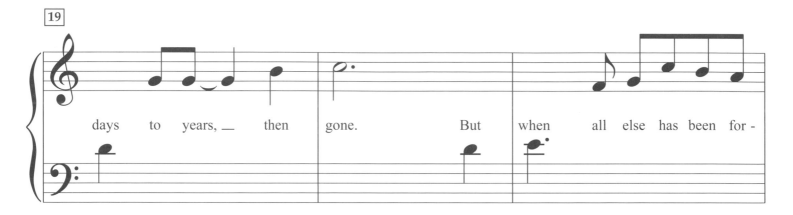

Remember Me
(Ernesto de la Cruz)
from COCO

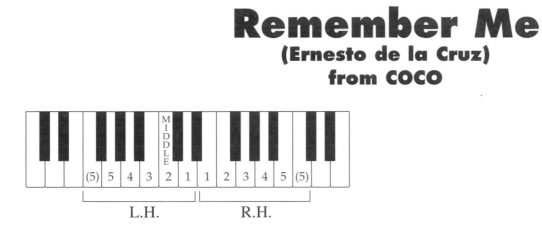

Music and Lyrics by Kristen Anderson-Lopez
and Robert Lopez

Re - mem - ber me, though I have to say good - bye. Re - mem - ber

me, don't let it make you cry. For e - ven if I'm far a - way, I

Duet Part (Student plays one octave higher than written.)

hold you in my heart. I sing a se - cret song to you each

night we are a - part. Re - mem - ber me though I

have to tra - vel far. Re - mem - ber me _____ each time you

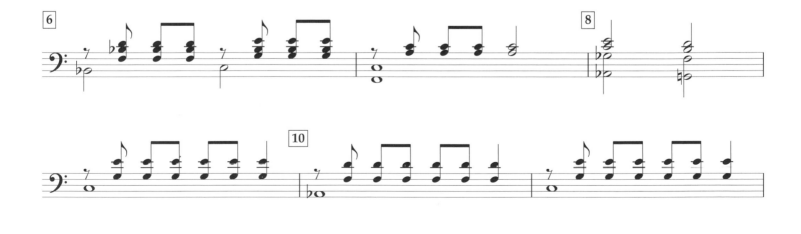

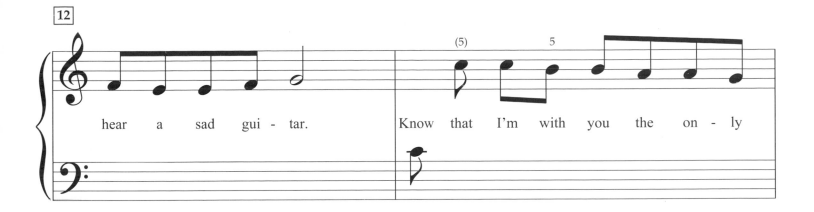

hear a sad gui - tar. Know that I'm with you the on - ly

way that I can be. Un - til you're in my arms a -

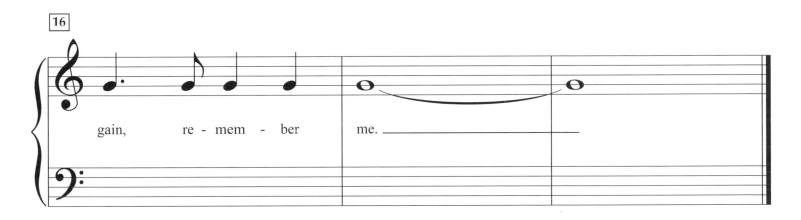

gain, re - mem - ber me. _____

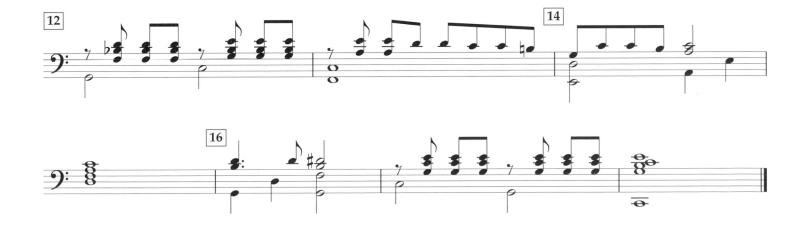

How Far I'll Go

from MOANA

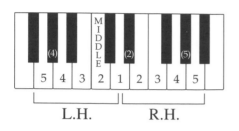

L.H.   R.H.

Music and Lyrics by
Lin-Manuel Miranda

Moderately

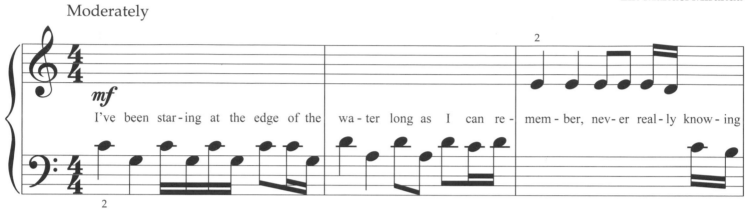

I've been star-ing at the edge of the wa-ter long as I can re-mem-ber, nev-er real-ly know-ing

why.   I wish I could be the per-fect daugh-ter, but I come back to the

Duet Part (Student plays one octave higher than written.)

Moderately

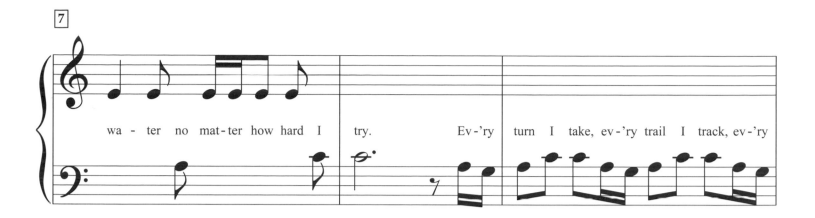

goes. _____ If the wind in my sail on the sea stays be-hind _____ me, one day I'll

know. _____ If I go, there's just no tell-ing how far I'll go. I know ev-'ry-bod-y on this

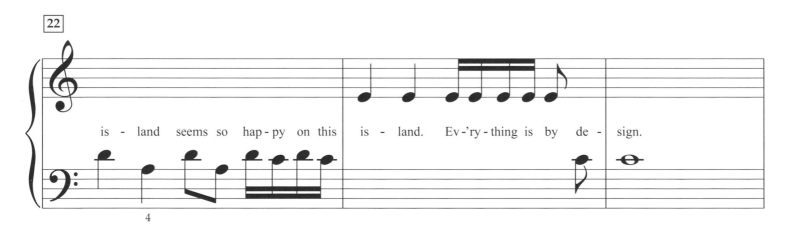

is - land seems so hap-py on this is - land. Ev-'ry-thing is by de - sign.

4

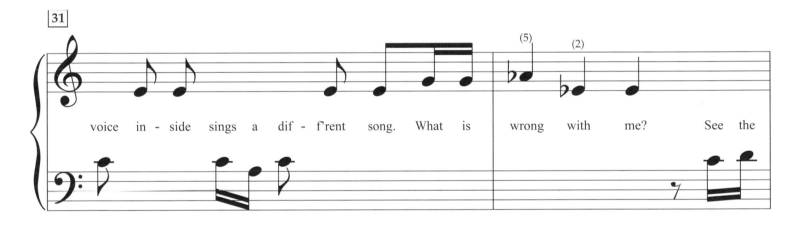

Un Poco Loco

from COCO

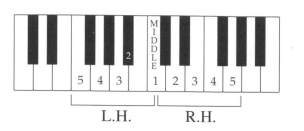

L.H.   R.H.

Music by Germaine Franco
Lyrics by Adrian Molina

Moderately, in 2, with a bounce

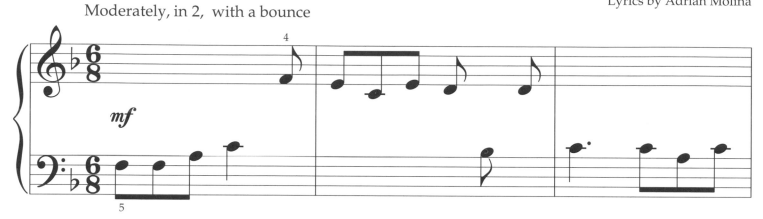

What col - or is the sky? Ay mi a-

Duet Part (Student plays one octave higher than written.)

Moderately, in 2, with a bounce

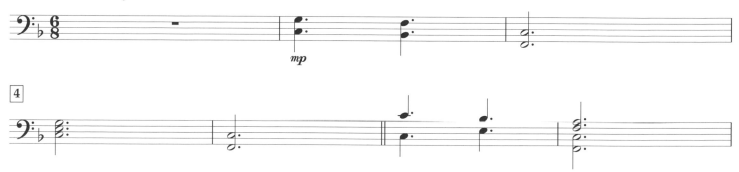

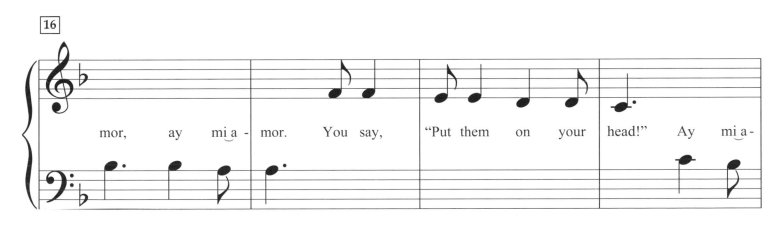

mor, ay mi a - mor. _____

You make me un po - co lo - co, ___ un po - qui - ti - ti - to

lo - co. ___ The way you keep me guess - ing, I'm ___

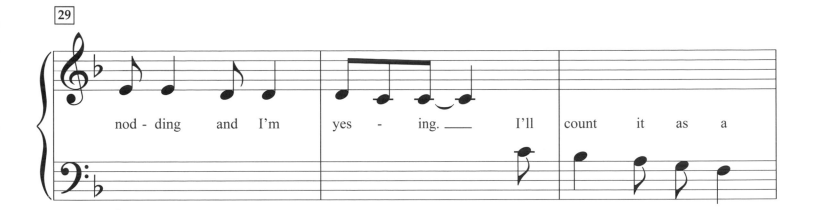

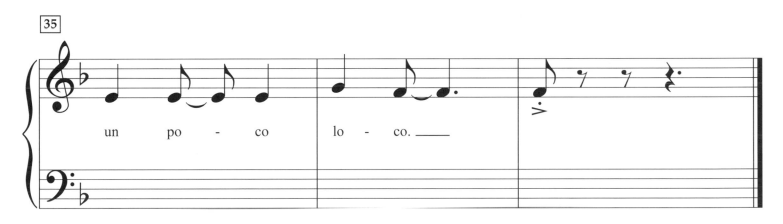

The World Es Mi Familia

from COCO

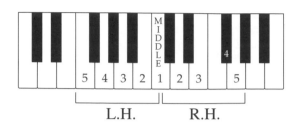

L.H.   R.H.

Music by Germaine Franco
Lyrics by Adrian Molina

Moderately fast, in 2

Se - ñor - as _____ y se - ñor - es, _____ bue - nas
tar - des, _____ bue - nas no - ches. _____ Bue - nas

Duet Part (Student plays one octave higher than written.)

Moderately fast, in 2

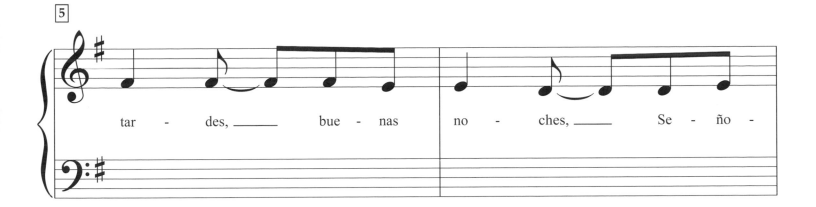

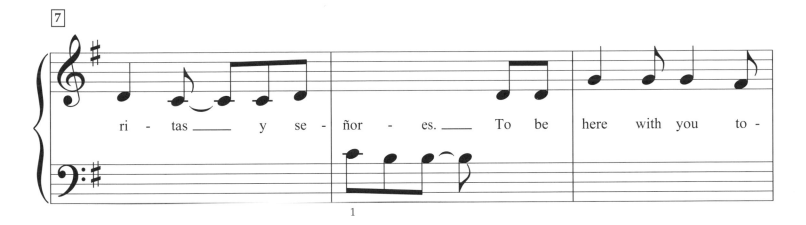

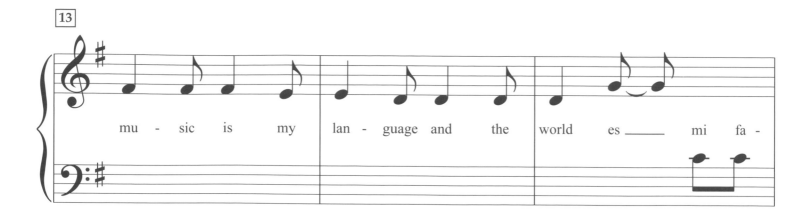

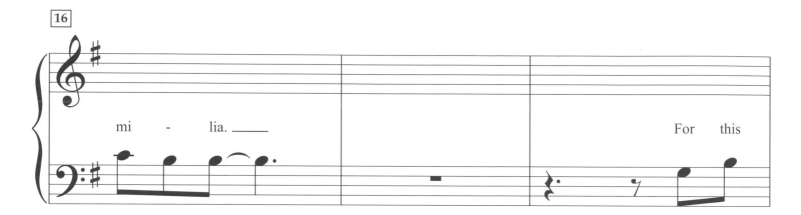

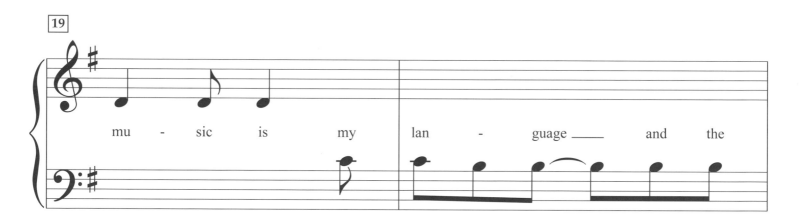

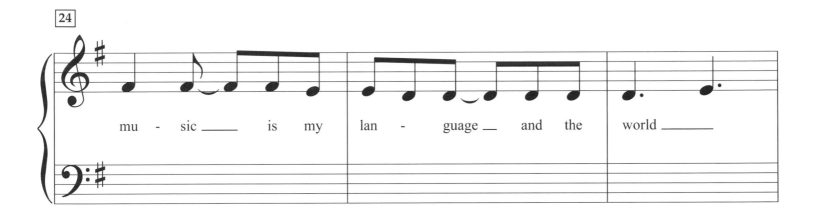

You're Welcome
from MOANA

Music and Lyrics by
Lin-Manuel Miranda

Duet Part (Student plays one octave higher than written.)

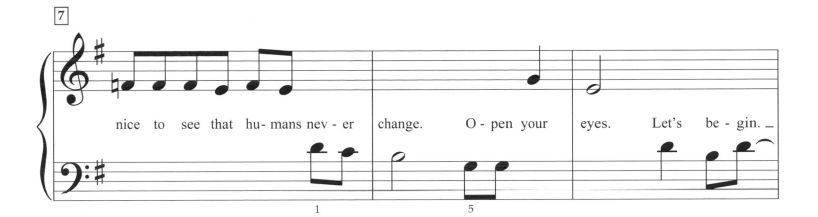

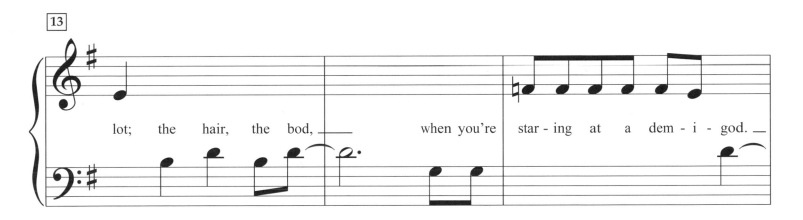

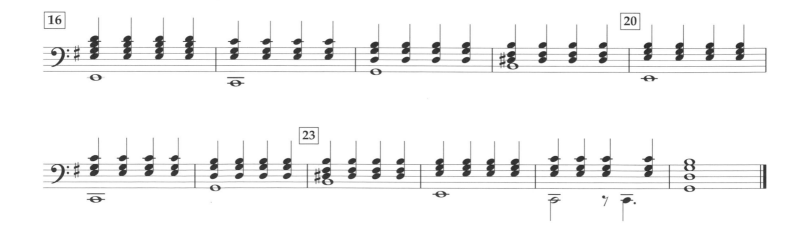